A Short-T

M000187205

INVITATION
P TO
SALMS

Abingdon Press
Nashville

A Short-Term DISCIPLE Bible Study

INVITATION TO PSALMS
LEADER GUIDE

Copyright © 2008 by Abingdon Press

This book is printed on recycled, acid-free, elemental chlorine-free paper.

Coin photo by Zev Radovan © Biblical Archaeological Society.

Judith Smith, Interim Editor of Church School Publications; Mark Price, Senior Editor; Mickey Frith, Associate Editor; Leo Ferguson, Designer; Marcia C'Debaca, Design Manager

08 09 10 11 12 13 14 15 16 17 — 10 9 8 7 6 5 4 3 2 1

MANUFACTURED IN THE UNITED STATES OF AMERICA

Contents

Introducing
This Study Series .

INVITATION TO PSALMS is one of a series of studies developed on the model of DISCIPLE Bible study. DISCIPLE is a family of Bible study resources based on the general assumption that people are hungry for God's Word, for fellowship in prayer and study, and for biblically informed guidance in ministry. Like all long-term DISCIPLE resources, this series of short-term DISCIPLE Bible studies: (1) presents the Bible as the primary text; (2) calls for daily preparation on the part of students; (3) features a weekly meeting based on small-group discussion; (4) includes a video component for making available the insights of biblical scholars to set the Scriptures in context; and (5) has as one of its goals the enhancement of Christian discipleship.

INVITATION TO PSALMS is designed to provide congregations with an in-depth, high-commitment Bible study resource able to be completed in a shorter time frame than the foundational DISCIPLE studies. However, the shorter time frame does not mean this study has expectations differ-ent from those associated with the thirty-four week DISCIPLE: BECOMING DISCIPLES THROUGH BIBLE STUDY. In fact, the term *invitation* rather than *introduction* has been used for this series to signal that these studies are not basic introductions but rather invitations to in-depth study. The expecta-tion remains that participants will prepare for the weekly meeting by read-ing substantial portions of Scripture and taking notes. The expectation remains that group discussion, rather than lecture, will be the preferred learning approach. The expectation remains that biblical scholarship will be part of the group's study together. The expectation remains that each person's encounter with the Bible will call him or her to more faithful dis-cipleship. In fact, it is our hope that this series of short-term DISCIPLE Bible studies will ultimately inspire participants to commit to a long-term DISCIPLE study in the future. For while these short studies of selected Scriptures can be both meaningful and convenient, the deeply transform-ing experience of reading and studying all the Scriptures—from Genesis to Revelation—continues to be the primary aim of DISCIPLE.

Leading This Study

For leaders of INVITATION TO PSALMS, it will be vital to keep in mind that to have as rich and meaningful an experience as possible with this type of short-term study, you will need to pay close attention to the timing of the suggested discussion activities and group dynamics. One of the challenges of any short-term, small-group study—especially one based on group discussion—is the time it takes for people in the study to become comfortable sharing with one another. If your group is made up of people who are already acquainted, the challenge may be minimal. However, be prepared to have a group of people who do not know each other well, perhaps some who have never done much substantive Bible study and others who are graduates of long-term DISCIPLE studies. Different challenges—and rewards—will come as a result of the mix of people who make up your group(s). Make use of the following information as you prepare to lead INVITATION TO PSALMS.

GROUP ORIENTATION

Plan to schedule an orientation meeting a week prior to the first weekly meeting. Take time then to make introductions, discuss the expectations of the study, distribute and review the materials, and preview the upcoming week's assignment. If necessary, consider discussing the kind of study Bible group members should use and taking time to make sure everyone is familiar with the aids in a study Bible. Have on hand several types of study Bibles for persons to look through.

WEEKLY SESSION

The times in parentheses beneath each section heading in the leader guide planning pages indicate the suggested number of minutes to allow for a particular activity. The first time is for use with a 60-minute meeting schedule, and the second time is for use with a 90-minute meeting schedule.

Keep in mind that the discussion questions suggested for use in any one section may be more than enough to take up the allotted time. You will need to keep an eye on a clock and decide when and whether to move on. **The best way to gauge in advance how many questions to use and how long to allow discussion to last is to spend time answering the suggested questions yourself while preparing for the group session.** Be sure to do this, as well as preview the video—both Part 1 and 2—before the weekly session.

Gathering Around God's Word

(5–10 minutes)

Welcome

Begin on time by welcoming the group to the study. Ideally, this should be the *second* time the group has been together. During the orientation meeting the previous week, group participants met to preview the materials, discuss expectations of the study, and receive the assignment for the week. In case group participants who were not present at the orientation meeting arrive at this first session, be prepared to summarize as briefly as possible what they can expect from the study and what the study will expect from them.

Prayer

Establish a particular ritual of praying together at the start of the study. Keep in mind that the text of this study, the Book of Psalms, is a treasury of prayers. Draw from it often. **Note also that the Session 3 commentary in the participant book deals with the Psalms as prayers, and it encourages students to practice praying the Psalms following a pattern outlined in the Book of Common Prayer.** Consider looking ahead at that session for ideas that might inform how your group prays together over the course of the study.

For those interested in a more visually creative suggestion, consider using the book *The Psalms: An Artist's Impression,* by Dutch painter Anneke Kaai and Eugene H. Peterson (InterVarsity Press, 1999). The oversized book is a collection of over twenty different works of art, very colorful and impressionistic and inspired by specific psalms. Each painting is accompanied by the psalm text that inspired it. All the psalms come from *The Message: The Bible in Contemporary Language,* the paraphrase of the Bible by Peterson. Consider using a psalm and its companion painting to open your group meetings in prayer and reflection.

Invitation From Scripture

At the close of the prayer time and just before introducing the first video segment, read aloud the focal verse of the session. The verse appears on the first page of each session in the participant book and is printed again in this section in the leader guide for each session. This reading is intended as an invitation to the session, serving to invoke God's presence and to give voice to the theme of the week's study. Consider reading aloud the focal verse from the TANAKH translation or from *The Message*.

Questions for Reflection

Follow up the reading aloud of the focal verse by presenting to the group the questions in this section. You may want to read them aloud, or you may print them on a white board or on a large sheet of paper for the group to see. Allow time for persons to consider the questions and then, if you choose, have them share briefly their responses in the total group. Another option would be to have persons reflect on the questions in silence and discuss them at the end of the meeting time.

Examining God's Word in Context

(20–30 minutes)

Viewing the Video: Part 1

The video component in the series has two parts, and both are central to the group's study. Part 1 of each video segment will present a particular psalm text (or texts) through both aural and visual expression. The aim of Part 1 is to help participants experience a specific psalm (always one listed in the week's reading assignments) through spoken word, music, and image. For example, in Session 8, Psalm 51 will be presented as a choral performance of Allegri's "Miserere," accompanied by the words of the text appearing on screen and illustrated by images of human faces. In fact, only in Session 8 do the words of the psalm appear on screen. All the other segments present the text of the psalm aurally, either spoken or sung.

Part 1 should serve as a time of personal reflection and meditation. The recommended procedure for using this video is as follows: (1) **Silence:** Group members should clear their minds in anticipation of receiving a new insight from a fresh hearing of God's Word. (2) **Listening:** Group members should listen carefully to the psalm as it is either spoken or sung, paying attention to how sound and image help convey the message of the text.

(3) **Discussion:** Thoughtful discussion should follow careful listening. Use the set of questions that appear in this section for guiding the group's responses.

Note: The length of each video segment is noted in parentheses at the start of the "Viewing the Video" sections. This information may help when planning the amount of time to allow for discussion.

Viewing the Video: Part 2

The focus in this section is on viewing Part 2 of the video. Part 2 of each video will feature insights from one of two biblical scholars, Julia O'Brien and Stephen Reid. The scholars will appear alternately in an informal interview format. They will talk about those psalms presented in the Part 1 segments, addressing such questions as:

- What can be inferred about the intent of the psalmist in this psalm?
- How might this psalm have been used by Israel in its worship?
- What does this psalm teach/say about God and God's relationship with people or the world?
- What particular characteristics of the psalm help articulate its message?

On its own, the conversation may prompt sufficient discussion by the group. Simply following up the video with questions such as "What insight from the scholar caught your attention and why?" or "How did the discussion inform your understanding of the week's reading?" may be enough to start and sustain a discussion. Another option is to choose one or more of the four general questions above to lead discussion, or simply use the bulleted follow-up questions that appear under "Discuss After Viewing Video."

Encountering God's Word in the Text

(20–25 minutes)

In this section, group discussion centers around the assigned Scripture passages read and studied during the week. **While this section features several sets of discussion questions or activities, keep in mind that the "Daily Assignments" sections in the participant book also suggest questions for reflection related to specific readings.** You might consider including those questions as part of group discussions, especially since participants will have seen and perhaps responded to those questions during their preparation.

During discussion, be alert for ways to make use of the information that appears throughout the commentary as marginal notes within a gray background image. That background image is in the shape of a silver coin minted during the Bar Kokhba Revolt (132–135 AD). The image depicts a lyre, a musical instrument used in Jewish worship and frequently mentioned in the Psalms.

Going Forth With God's Word: An Invitation to Discipleship

(15–20 minutes)

Consideration of the implications of the week's readings for Christian discipleship is the point of this section. The discussion questions in the leader guide for each session come from questions raised in the commentary and the "For Reflection" sections of the participant book. Be alert to additional questions that come to mind and might be useful at this time in the group meeting. As with any of these discussion questions, some will work better than others, and some will take more time to answer than others. Given the time frame for your weekly meeting, you may not have time to work through all the questions in the leader guide. Choose those you think will work best for your group, or make up your own.

Closing and Prayer

Turn to the next session and preview the lesson and assignments for the week ahead. Establish a pattern of inviting prayer concerns and praying together at this time.

GROUP DYNAMICS

The effectiveness of the group's study together depends heavily upon the way you as the leader manage individual participation. Plan for the majority of the weekly discussion to take place in smaller groups of two to four. Smaller groupings will give everyone more opportunity to talk and are the best way for people to get to know one another quickly. They also reduce the possibility that a couple of people will dominate the conversation or that some will not contribute at all. Smaller groupings communicate that preparation is expected and essential for fruitful discussion.

Also key to the effectiveness of the group's study together is how you manage your role as the leader. Remember that your primary role is to facilitate the process, not to provide the information. To that end, follow these basic guidelines as you lead the study:

- Prepare exactly as participants would prepare; see yourself as a learner among learners.

- Know where the discussion is heading from the outset; this will minimize the chances of getting sidetracked along the way.

- Set ground rules for group participation and maintenance early on; doing so will encourage the whole group to take responsibility for monitoring itself.

- Be a good listener; don't be afraid of silence. Allow time for people to think before responding.

Additional Resources

Your group will need only the Bible and the participant book to have a meaningful experience with this study. However, if your group should encounter unfamiliar terms and concepts or would like more information about some biblical text or topic, be prepared to suggest or to bring in additional reference materials for them to use. You may choose to include additional research or study activities in your plan for the weekly meeting, or you may assign group members to make use of these other reference materials outside of the meeting time and to report briefly to the group.

Several resources—including versions in print and CD-ROM—are recommended as follows:

Bibles

One of the ways to enhance people's reading and understanding of the Bible is to have them read from more than one translation. Plan to have several study Bible versions available in the meeting room. In addition, encourage your group to read the Bible with curiosity, to ask *Who? What? Where? When? How?* and *Why?* as they read. Remind your group to let the Scripture speak for itself, even if the apparent meaning is troubling or unclear. Affirm both asking questions of Scripture as well as seeking answers to those questions in Scripture itself.

Bible Dictionaries
- *Eerdmans Dictionary of the Bible*, edited by David Noel Freedman (William B. Eerdmans Publishing Company, 2000).
- *Eerdmans Commentary on the Bible*, edited by James D. G. Dunn and John W. Rogerson (William B. Eerdmans Publishing Company, 2003).

Introductory Resources
- *Understanding the Old Testament*, abridged fourth edition, by Bernhard W. Anderson with Katheryn Pfisterer Darr (Prentice-Hall, Inc., 1997).
- *Answering God: The Psalms as Tools for Prayer*, by Eugene Peterson (HarperSanFrancisco, 1989).
- *The Biblical Psalms in Christian Worship: A Brief Introduction and Guide to Resources*, by John D. Witvliet (William B. Eerdmans Publishing Company, 2007).

Biblical Commentaries
- *The Message of the Psalms: A Theological Commentary*, by Walter Brueggemann (Augsburg Press, 1984).
- *The New Interpreter's Bible: A Commentary in Twelve Volumes*, Vol. IV, the commentary on Psalms (Abingdon Press, 1996). Also available in a CD-ROM edition.
- *In the House of the Lord: Inhabiting the Psalms of Lament*, by Michael Jinkins (The Liturgical Press, 1998).
- *Listening In: A Multicultural Reading of the Psalms*, by Stephen Breck Reid (Abingdon Press, 1997).

Art and Archaeology Related to the Bible
- *Archaeological Study Bible*, New International Version (The Zondervan Corporation, 2005).
- *The Biblical World in Pictures*, revised edition, CD-ROM (Biblical Archaeological Society).
- *The Psalms: An Artist's Impression*, by Anneke Kaai and Eugene H. Peterson (InterVarsity Press, 1999).
- *Psalms: The Saint John's Bible*, handwritten and illuminated by Donald Jackson (The Liturgical Press, 2006).

Word of God, Words of Prayer

Gathering Around God's Word

(5–10 minutes)

Welcome

Begin on time by welcoming the group to the study. Ideally this should be the second time the group has been together. During the orientation meeting the previous week, group participants met to preview the material, discuss expectations of the study, and receive the assignment for the week. In case group participants who were not present at the orientation meeting arrive at the first session, be prepared to summarize as briefly as possible what they can expect from the study and what the study will expect from them.

Prayer

Establish a particular ritual of praying together at the start of the study. Keep in mind that the text of this study, the Book of Psalms, is a treasury of prayers. Draw from it often. For this session, consider using Psalm 13.

If you are interested in a more visually creative suggestion, consider using the book *The Psalms: An Artist's Impression*, by Dutch painter Anneke Kaai and Eugene H. Peterson (InterVarsity Press, 1999). The oversized book is a collection of over twenty different works of art, very colorful and impressionistic, inspired by specific psalms. Each painting is accompanied by the psalm text that inspired it. All the psalms come from *The Message: The Bible in Contemporary Language*, the contemporary paraphrase of the Bible by Peterson. Try using a psalm and its companion painting to open this week's group meeting in prayer and reflection.

Invitation From Scripture

But you, O LORD, are a shield around me / my glory, and the one who lifts up my head. / I cry aloud to the LORD, / and he answers me from his holy hill.
—*Psalm 3:3-4*

Questions for Reflection

- As you begin this study, what words would you use to characterize the Psalms and what they mean to you?
- At what particular times in your life have you found yourself turning to the Psalms? Why the Psalms?

Examining God's Word in Context

(20–30 minutes)

The Psalms serve as the ultimate spiritual cathartic for the revenge-ravaged soul and the ultimate antidote to the spiritual denial that afflicts us.

Viewing the Video: Session 1, Part 1 (3:35)

The video component in the series has two parts, and both are central to the group's study. Part 1 of each video segment will present a particular psalm text (or texts) through both aural and visual expression. The aim of Part 1 is to help participants experience a specific psalm (always one listed in the week's reading assignments) through spoken word, music, and image and then invite both reflection and discussion. The recommended procedure for using this video is as follows: (1) **Preparation**: Group members should clear their minds in anticipation of receiving a new insight from a fresh hearing of God's Word. (2) **Attention**: Group members should listen meditatively to the psalm text (or texts) as they are presented either by recitation or through music, and pay attention to the images and how they illuminate the text of the psalm(s). (3) **Discussion**: Thoughtful discussion should follow careful listening. Use the following set of questions for guiding the group's responses.

Psalms 1 & 23

- After viewing this video segment, what would you say is the basic message of each of these psalms?
- What thoughts or feelings were evoked by the music and images that accompanied these two psalms?
- Where in the context of worship would you expect to hear these psalms recited or sung? Why?

- When in your life have you found these psalms most meaningful?

Viewing the Video: Session 1, Part 2 (5:46)

The focus in this section is on viewing Part 2 of the video. Part 2 of each video will feature insights from one of two biblical scholars, Julia O'Brien and Stephen Reid. The scholars will appear alternately in an informal interview format. They will talk about those psalms presented in the Part 1 segments, addressing such questions as:

- What can be inferred about the intent of the psalmist in each of these psalms?

- How might these psalms have been used by Israel in its worship?

- What do these psalms teach/say about God and God's relationship with people or the world?

- What particular characteristics of these psalms help articulate their message?

Prepare to View Video

The Psalms call us to bring all aspects of human life consciously into the presence of God in prayer. Listen for what the psalms say about God and God's relationship with people or the world.

Discuss After Viewing Video

In this video segment, Old Testament scholar Julia O'Brien discusses Psalm 1 and Psalm 23. On its own, the conversation may prompt sufficient discussion by the group. Simply following up the video with questions such as "What insight from the scholar caught your attention and why?" or "How did the discussion inform your understanding of the week's reading?" may be enough to start and sustain a discussion. Another option is to choose one or more of the four general questions above to prompt discussion of the video, or consider using the questions below:

- Noting the imagery found in Psalm 1, what can be said about the path of the righteous? The path of the unrighteous? How does the church define these two paths today?

- How does Psalm 1 prepare us for the reading of the Book of Psalms? What is your understanding of "the law of the LORD" and its impact on the life of faith? When you consider the idea of God's law, do you think of it as a burden or a delight? Why?

- How does Psalm 23 bring you comfort in contemplating both life and death?

Encountering God's Word in the Text

(20–30 minutes)

The readings this week introduce us to the Book of Psalms and the range of prayers they exemplify. Form three groups as indicated below:

Group 1: Day 2 readings

Group 2: Day 3 readings

Group 3: Day 5 readings

Examine the readings for that day looking for the following: (1) the image of humanity depicted by the psalmists; (2) the image of God depicted by the psalmists; and (3) the Word of God the psalmists proclaim.

Allow the three groups an opportunity to share briefly their findings. Then in those smaller groups of three or four, discuss the following questions:

- Consider this statement: "The Word of God never exists hermetically sealed in isolation from human history" (participant book, page 17). In light of that claim, how would you define *the Word of God*? How would you define *prayer*?

- Based on your own prayer life, what is your predominant image of God? How does your image of God compare to the image(s) portrayed in the psalms you read this week?

The Scripture reading for Day 4 is Psalm 23. One of the suggestions in the daily assignment is to read Psalm 22 and then read Psalm 23 immediately after. Try that as a group. Enlist several persons to read aloud Psalm 22 and then Psalm 23, with only a brief pause in between, from different translations (for example, the King James Version, New International Version, New Jerusalem Bible, Contemporary English Version). Then share responses to the question "Why do you think those who assembled the Book of Psalms placed these psalms next to one another?" (participant book, page 16).

Going Forth With God's Word: An Invitation to Discipleship

(15–20 minutes)

We cannot read the Psalms without risking a deeper involvement in the life of faith; and we cannot pray them without risking the loss of our hearts to God's reign. In pairs, discuss the following questions:

- The sense of God's absence in the Psalms brings the psalmist to the point of despair. When have you experienced God's absence? How did it feel? How did you respond?

- God's faithfulness is portrayed in various ways in the Psalms. In your own life, how would you characterize God's faithfulness?

- What do you think Bonhoeffer means by saying, "It does not matter whether the Psalms express exactly what we feel in our heart at the moment we pray. Perhaps it is precisely the case that we must pray against our own heart in order to pray rightly"* (participant book, page 20)? When has that been your experience of the Psalms?

Call attention to the "For Reflection" section on page 21 in the participant book. Ask pairs to share responses to the questions.

Closing and Prayer

Turn to Session 2, and review the focus of the lesson and the assignments for the week ahead. Establish a pattern of inviting prayer concerns and praying together at this time.

---

* From *Prayerbook of the Bible: An Introduction to the Psalms*, by Dietrich Bonhoeffer, in Dietrich Bonhoeffer Works, Vol. 5, translated by James H. Burtness (Fortress Press, 1996); page 157.

The Prayer Book of God's People

Gathering Around God's Word

(5–10 minutes)

Welcome

Begin on time by welcoming the group to the study.

Prayer

Pray together as you begin your study. Consider using some of the prayers recorded in the Psalms, such as Psalm 113.

Invitation From Scripture

Blessed be the name of the LORD / from this time on and forevermore. / From the rising of the sun to its setting / the name of the LORD is to be praised.

—Psalm 113:2-3

Questions for Reflection

- To what extent would you say your prayers express your faith?

- What specific words, phrases, patterns, or expressions recur in how you pray?

Examining God's Word in Context

(20–30 minutes)

The biblical psalms inspired and provided the fundamental forms of praise used in the development of Christian hymnody.

Viewing the Video: Session 2, Part 1 (3:08)

The aim of Part 1 is to help participants experience a specific psalm (always one listed in the week's reading assignments) through spoken word, music, and image and then invite both reflection and discussion. The recommended procedure for using this video is as follows: (1) **Preparation:**

Group members should clear their minds in anticipation of receiving a new insight from a fresh hearing of God's Word. (2) **Attention:** Group members should listen meditatively to the psalm text (or texts) as they are presented either by recitation or through music, and pay attention to the images and how they illuminate the text of the psalm(s). (3) **Discussion:** Thoughtful discussion should follow careful listening. Use the following set of questions for guiding the group's responses.

Psalm 136
- After viewing this video segment, what would you say is the basic message of this psalm?

- What thoughts or feelings were evoked by the music and images that accompanied this psalm?

- Where in the context of worship would you expect to hear this psalm recited or sung? Why?

- When in your life have you found this psalm most meaningful?

Viewing the Video: Session 2, Part 2 (5:30)
The focus in this section is on viewing Part 2 of the video. Part 2 of each video will feature insights from one of two biblical scholars who will appear alternately in an informal interview format. They will talk about those psalms presented in the Part 1 segments, addressing such questions as:

- What can be inferred about the intent of the psalmist in this psalm?

- How might this psalm have been used by Israel in its worship?

- What does this psalm teach/say about God and God's relationship with people or the world?

- What particular characteristics of the psalm help articulate its message?

Prepare to View Video
Listen for what is said about the importance of liturgical memory in a psalm like Psalm 136, both for the people of Israel and for God's people today.

Discuss After Viewing Video
In this video segment, Old Testament scholar Stephen Reid discusses Psalm 136. On its own, the conversation may prompt sufficient discussion by the group. Simply following up the video with questions such as

"What insight from the scholar caught your attention and why?" or "How did the discussion inform your understanding of the week's reading?" may be enough to start and sustain a discussion. Another option is to choose one or more of the four general questions above to prompt discussion of the video, or consider using the questions below:

- The Psalms often seem so personal. How do you see the message of the Psalms effective in the formation of community?

- In what way are the events in the story of God's people highlighted in Psalm 136 also part of the church's story? What other events would you include in this list?

- What are the characteristics that separate God from false gods? How are these characteristics portrayed in the Psalms?

Encountering God's Word in the Text

(20–30 minutes)

The Psalms as prayers respond to the Word who is God, and in their response the Psalms become the Word of God to us. Praying the Psalms draws us into this profound conversation.

Form four groups to explore some of the assigned Scriptures. Assign the readings in this manner:

Group 1: Day 2 readings

Group 2: Day 3 readings

Group 3: Day 4 readings

Group 4: Day 5 readings

Ask the groups to recall the readings, scan any notes made during their preparation, and then discuss the following questions:

- What do the assigned psalm and the psalm/prayer/song outside the Book of Psalms have in common? How are they different?

In the total group, invite each person to recall how he or she answered the question in the assignment for Day 1 (participant book, page 24): "When you know God has acted in your life, how do you usually respond?" Allow time to share responses around the group. Then ask everyone to reflect for a moment about the God who acts, the God who is worthy to be praised, the God whose steadfast love endures forever.

After allowing time for reflection, ask everyone to come up with a specific phrase that describes the God they have been contemplating. Have them jot it down on a piece of paper. This phrase should begin with the word *who* (for example, "who cares for all people"). Once everyone has a phrase, have the group stand in a circle. Then go around the circle, with each person reading aloud his or her phrase in this fashion:

1. First the total group says in unison, "O give thanks to the God of gods...."

2. Then one person reads aloud his or her phrase, "who...."

3. After that person reads his or her phrase, the whole group again speaks aloud, saying, "for his steadfast love endures forever."

Follow this recitation pattern until everyone has had a chance to voice his or her phrase describing God.

Going Forth With God's Word: An Invitation to Discipleship

(15–20 minutes)

The Psalms invite their readers into the practice of giving expression to our faith out of the deep wells of ancient faith expressed within the Bible. In pairs, discuss the following questions:

- On what occasions has the language of the psalmists been your own personal prayer language?

- When was the last time you prayed specifically for someone or when someone prayed specifically for you? What happened?

- Call attention to the "For Reflection" section on page 32 in the participant book. Ask pairs to share responses to the questions.

Closing and Prayer

Turn to Session 3, and review the focus of the lesson and the assignments for the week ahead. Invite prayer concerns and pray together at this time.

Praying the Psalms

Gathering Around God's Word

(5–10 minutes)

Welcome
Begin on time by welcoming the group to the study.

Prayer
Pray together as you begin your study. Consider using some of the prayers recorded in the Psalms, such as Psalm 103.

Invitation From Scripture
To you, O LORD, I lift up my soul. / O my God, in you I trust. —Psalm 25:1

Questions for Reflection
- How would you describe your practice of reading specific psalms morning and evening over the past week? Could you commit to reading all 150 Psalms over the course of a month? Why or why not?

- What makes disciplined practices such as reading the Bible twice a day so difficult a challenge for many people today?

Examining God's Word in Context

(20–30 minutes)

Viewing the Video: Session 3, Part 1 (3:52)
The aim of Part 1 is to help participants experience a specific psalm (always one listed in the week's reading assignments) through spoken word, music, and image and then invite both reflection and discussion. The recommended procedure for using this video is as follows: (1) **Preparation:** Group members should clear their minds in anticipation of receiving a new insight from a fresh hearing of God's Word. (2) **Attention:** Group members should listen meditatively to the psalm text (or texts) as they are presented

either by recitation or through music, and pay attention to the images and how they illuminate the text of the psalm(s). (3) **Discussion:** Thoughtful discussion should follow careful listening. Use the following set of questions for guiding the group's responses.

Psalms 42 & 43

- After viewing this video segment, what would you say is the basic message of each of these psalms?

- What thoughts or feelings were evoked by the music and images that accompanied these psalms?

- Where in the context of worship would you expect to hear these psalms recited or sung? Why?

- When in your life have you found these psalms most meaningful?

Viewing the Video: Session 3, Part 2 (5:28)

The focus in this section is on viewing Part 2 of the video. Part 2 of each video will feature insights from one of two biblical scholars who will appear alternately in an informal interview format. They will talk about those psalms presented in the Part 1 segments, addressing such questions as:

- What can be inferred about the intent of the psalmist in this psalm?

- How might this psalm have been used by Israel in its worship?

- What does this psalm teach/say about God and God's relationship with people or the world?

- What particular characteristics of the psalm help articulate its message?

Prepare to View Video

Listen for what is said about the particularity of the context of Psalms 42 and 43 and how readers today can still find relevance in the Psalms' message.

Discuss After Viewing Video

In this video segment, Old Testament scholar Julia O'Brien discusses Psalm 42 and Psalm 43. On its own, the conversation may prompt sufficient discussion by the group. Simply following up the video with questions such as "What insight from the scholar caught your attention and why?" or "How did the discussion inform your understanding of the week's reading?" may be enough to start and sustain a discussion. Another option is to choose one or more of the four general questions above to prompt discussion of the video, or consider using the questions below:

- According to Dr. O'Brien, the combined Psalms 42 and 43 are a song about longing, particularly longing to be in a place where God is. When have you ever experienced that kind of longing? What image would you use to describe it?

- In light of the example of Psalms 42 and 43, what makes the words and images in an ancient text like the Psalms still meaningful to modern readers?

Encountering God's Word in the Text

(20–30 minutes)

In order to understand the Psalms on their own terms, we must pray them. Form groups of three or four, and have each person select a psalm from this week's assigned readings. Have the groups first pray each of the selected psalms, one by one, and then discuss the message of those psalms.

In the total group, read aloud Psalm 63. Instruct everyone to listen and pay particular attention to the sensory images in the text. Then talk about what scents, tastes, sights, and sounds Psalm 63 evoked.

Finally, lead the total group in a guided prayer using Psalm 23 in the following way:

The LORD is my shepherd, I shall not want.
    (Think of a time when your needs were met.)
He makes me lie down in green pastures;
    (Where do you go to find quiet and peace?)
he leads me beside still waters;
    (Where do you have to go or what do you have to do to slow down?)
he restores my soul.
    (What have you found to be the best way to revive your spirit?)
He leads me in right paths for his name's sake.
    (Who has been an influence to you in your walk of faith, and how did he or she go about it?)
Even though I walk through the darkest valley,
    (Think of the most difficult time in your life.)

I fear no evil; for you are with me;
    (What do you fear?)
your rod and your staff—they comfort me.
    (What brings you comfort?)
You prepare a table before me in the presence of my enemies;
    (Who is present at the table? What is their reaction? What is
    yours?)
you anoint my head with oil;
    (Think of a time when someone cared for you.)
my cup overflows.
    (Think of a moment when your joy has been full.)
Surely goodness and mercy shall follow me all the days of my life,
    (How does it feel knowing that mercy is behind you?)
and I shall dwell in the house of the LORD my whole life long.
    (Think of going home, the joy of getting there, and the smiles of
    loved ones coming out to greet you.)

Going Forth With God's Word: An Invitation to Discipleship

(15–20 minutes)

The Christian discipline of praying the Psalms daily offers an especially potent practice that depends on the extent to which we find time to do nothing else but pray.

- When do you find is the best time for you to pause for a moment of prayer? What would it take for you to increase the time you spend in prayer? What interruptions would you have to address? How might praying the Psalms help you in making time to pray?

- If prayer is a conversation with God, what kind of conversations do you have with God these days? In what way do you allow God to talk with you?

Call attention to the "For Reflection" section on page 47 in the participant book. Ask pairs to share responses to the questions.

Closing and Prayer

Turn to Session 4, and review the focus of the lesson and the assignments for the week ahead. Invite prayer concerns and pray together at this time.

The Language of the Heart

Gathering Around God's Word

(5–10 minutes)

Welcome

Begin on time by welcoming the group to the study.

Prayer

Pray together as you begin your study. Consider using some of the prayers recorded in the Psalms, such as Psalm 90.

Invitation From Scripture

The LORD is your keeper; / the LORD is your shade at your right hand. / The sun shall not strike you by day, / nor the moon by night. —Psalm 121:5-6

Questions for Reflection

- To what extent does the poetry of the Psalms speak from and to your feelings—that is, your heart?

- What kind of words or speech do you use to communicate to God out of your heart?

Examining God's Word in Context

(20–30 minutes)

If we want to hear the Psalms in all their depth and subtleties, we must understand that <u>life is lived in rhythms,</u> like the beat of a heart.

Viewing the Video: Session 4, Part 1 (5:35)

The aim of Part 1 is to help participants experience a specific psalm (always one listed in the week's reading assignments) through spoken word, music, and image and then invite both reflection and discussion. The recommended procedure for using this video is as follows: (1) **Preparation:**

Group members should clear their minds in anticipation of receiving a new insight from a fresh hearing of God's Word. (2) **Attention:** Group members should listen meditatively to the psalm text (or texts) as they are presented either by recitation or through music, and pay attention to the images and how they illuminate the text of the psalm(s). (3) **Discussion:** Thoughtful discussion should follow careful listening. Use the following set of questions for guiding the group's responses.

Note: *In this video segment, the text of Psalm 27 is a plainsong chant version. It differs from the NRSV.*

Psalm 27

- After viewing this video segment, what would you say is the basic message of this psalm?

- What thoughts or feelings were evoked by the music and images that accompanied the psalm?

- Where in the context of worship would you expect to hear this psalm recited or sung? Why?

- When in your life have you found this psalm most meaningful?

Viewing the Video: Session 4, Part 2 (5:37)

The focus in this section is on viewing Part 2 of the video. Part 2 of each video will feature insights from one of two biblical scholars who will appear alternately in an informal interview format. They will talk about those psalms presented in the Part 1 segments, addressing such questions as:

- What can be inferred about the intent of the psalmist in this psalm?

- How might this psalm have been used by Israel in its worship?

- What does this psalm teach/say about God and God's relationship with people or the world?

- What particular characteristics of the psalm help articulate its message?

Prepare to View Video

Listen for what is said about the fear expressed by the psalmist and about the notion of God as "patron."

Discuss After Viewing Video

In this video segment, Old Testament scholar Stephen Reid discusses Psalm 27. On its own, the conversation may prompt sufficient discussion by the group. Simply following up the video with questions such as "What insight from the scholar caught your attention and why?" or "How did the discussion inform your understanding of the week's reading?" may be enough to start and sustain a discussion. Another option is to choose one or more of the four general questions above to prompt discussion of the video, or consider using the questions below:

- Fear is a strong emotion that can lead to action or dysfunction. How is fear described in the Psalms? What do the Psalms prescribe to overcome fear? What tends to be your way of handling fear?

- How is it possible to see the world from God's perspective? What impact would having this kind of vision have on the church? On each of us?

Encountering God's Word in the Text

(20–30 minutes)

The Psalms invite us to taste and see that the Lord is good by beholding the beauty and relishing the flavor of words that convey the Word of God.

Form four groups and assign them the following psalms to study together:

Group 1: Psalm 38

Group 2: Psalm 116

Group 3: Psalm 37

Group 4: Psalm 103

The purpose of the groups' study is to examine the psalm's poetic imagery. Discussion in each group should focus on identifying what images the psalmist uses and how they function to convey the message of the psalm. Then, based on the imagery identified in the psalm, each group should develop a description of a person who might have been the inspiration for the psalm. For instance:

- Who is the person crying out to God in Psalm 38?

- What is that person like?

- What could be the nature of his or her suffering?

Then, with a description of this person and the person's situation in mind, each group should come up with a paraphrase of the psalm, trying to express in contemporary language this imagined person's prayer to God.

Allow time for each group to share its paraphrase. Then as a total group, discuss the following questions:

- How do the psalms in this week's readings reflect the rhythm of human life?

- What language of the heart is communicated through these Psalms?

Read Psalm 29 aloud. Before you begin, ask persons to listen for images of "the voice of the LORD" as the psalm is read. Following the reading, discuss the following questions:

- What images of the voice of the Lord did you find most striking or meaningful?

- Based on the imagery in this psalm, how would you describe the psalmist's concept or understanding of God?

Going Forth With God's Word: An Invitation to Discipleship

(15–20 minutes)

The Psalms call us to "be still" so that new understandings can work their way quietly into our hearts.

- What is your image of God, and how does that image shape the way you pray to God?

- Which of the psalms you read this past week most resonated with you or most nearly reflected your feelings at the time?

Call attention to the "For Reflection" section on page 58 in the participant book. Ask pairs to share responses to the questions.

Closing and Prayer

Turn to Session 5, and review the focus of the lesson and the assignments for the week ahead. Invite prayer concerns and pray together at this time.

A Geography of the Imagination

Gathering Around God's Word

(5–10 minutes)

Welcome
Begin on time by welcoming the group to the study.

Prayer
Pray together as you begin your study. Consider using some of the prayers recorded in the Psalms, such as Psalm 77.

Invitation From Scripture
The heavens are telling the glory of God; / and the firmament proclaims his handiwork. / Day to day pours forth speech, / and night to night declares knowledge. / There is no speech, nor are there words; / their voice is not heard; / yet their voice goes out through all the earth, / and their words to the end of the world.

—Psalm 19:1-4

Questions for Reflection
- In the readings this week, what were the most striking images from nature the psalmists used to depict God? What do you think the psalmists intended to say about God?

- What images come to mind in the history of Israel that best illustrate God's faithfulness? What life experiences most affect your image of God and of God's faithfulness?

Examining God's Word in Context

(20–30 minutes)

The images of nature in the Psalms are intended to serve as a portal to a deeper understanding of God, reminding us that nature is good because God created it.

Viewing the Video: Session 5, Part 1 (3:25)

The aim of Part 1 is to help participants experience a specific psalm (always one listed in the week's reading assignments) through spoken word, music, and image and then invite both reflection and discussion. The recommended procedure for using this video is as follows: (1) **Preparation:** Group members should clear their minds in anticipation of receiving a new insight from a fresh hearing of God's Word. (2) **Attention:** Group members should listen meditatively to the psalm text (or texts) as they are presented either by recitation or through music, and pay attention to the images and how they illuminate the text of the psalm(s). (3) **Discussion:** Thoughtful discussion should follow careful listening. Use the following set of questions for guiding the group's responses.

Psalm 19

- After viewing this video segment, what would you say is the basic message of this psalm?

- What thoughts or feelings were evoked by the music and images that accompanied the psalm?

- Where in the context of worship would you expect to hear this psalm recited or sung? Why?

- When in your life have you found this psalm most meaningful?

Viewing the Video: Session 5, Part 2 (4:10)

The focus in this section is on viewing Part 2 of the video. Part 2 of each video will feature insights from one of two biblical scholars who will appear alternately in an informal interview format. They will talk about those psalms presented in the Part 1 segments, addressing such questions as:

- What can be inferred about the intent of the psalmist in this psalm?

- How might this psalm have been used by Israel in its worship?

- What does this psalm teach/say about God and God's relationship with people or the world?

- What particular characteristics of the psalm help articulate its message?

Prepare to View Video

Listen for what is said about how the poetry of Psalm 19 integrates praise of God's creation with the celebration of God's instruction.

31

Discuss After Viewing Video

In this video segment, Old Testament scholar Julia O'Brien discusses Psalm 19. On its own, the conversation may prompt sufficient discussion by the group. Simply following up the video with questions such as "What insight from the scholar caught your attention and why?" or "How did the discussion inform your understanding of the week's reading?" may be enough to start and sustain a discussion. Another option is to choose one or more of the four general questions above to prompt discussion of the video, or consider using the questions below:

- How do you normally see the biblical concepts of Creation and Law as distinct from or related to each other? Why is that?

- Why do you think the psalmist wants to emphasize God's law as a part of the created order?

- What do you think of when you hear or recite Psalm 19:14?

Encountering God's Word in the Text

(20–30 minutes)

Our life with God is a life with both feet planted on a certain patch of ground, among a very specific community of people, and at a precise moment in history.

Hear Psalm 46 read aloud. Following the reading, distribute hymnals to everyone in your study group and sing (or recite) together the hymn "A Mighty Fortress Is Our God."

Form groups of three or four to explore the week's assigned psalms within the context of your church's hymnbook. Ask groups to look back over the psalms they read during the week. Then have the groups look through the hymnal to find hymns or specific hymn stanzas that declare certain attributes of God through images of nature. Talk together about how the church can celebrate the attributes of God through nature and life experiences.

Part of the Scripture reading for Day 5 was Psalm 137 and 2 Kings 24 and 25. As a group, read 2 Kings 25:1-21, then Psalm 137. With these Scriptures as a backdrop, share responses to the first set of questions listed under the "For Reflection" section of the participant book, page 68: "Why is it significant that the Bible connects the worship of God with the history of God's people? What implications might there be for your own experience of worship?"

Then, as a total group, read aloud Psalm 106. After listening to the psalm, consider these questions together:

- How does the church make the events of Israel's exodus and exile a part of its own story?

- How does your congregation celebrate the past, link it to the present, and against that backdrop, celebrate the faithfulness of God?

In the total group, sing together the hymn "Blessed Be the Name."

Going Forth With God's Word: An Invitation to Discipleship

(15–20 minutes)

The Psalms remind us that God is at work through all this human activity, all this apparently historical movement, in order to keep us from crafting our own likeness into an object of worship, and thus transform us into the likeness of Christ.

- What hymn or song communicates your own experience of God's faithfulness?

- What event in your life can you remember that enables you to affirm God's faithfulness?

- Which of the following features in nature characterizes where you are in your walk of faith and why? **The Grand Canyon. A gentle flowing stream. A rushing river. A stagnant pond. The Sahara Desert. The ocean. A sapling in a forest of trees.** Others?

Call attention to the "For Reflection" section on page 68 in the participant book. Ask pairs to share responses to the last three sets of questions.

Closing and Prayer

Turn to Session 6, and review the focus of the lesson and the assignments for the week ahead. Invite prayer concerns and pray together at this time.

A Theology of the Imagination

(5–10 minutes)

Welcome

Begin on time by welcoming the group to the study.

Prayer

Pray together as you begin your study. Consider using some of the prayers recorded in the Psalms, such as Psalm 95.

Invitation From Scripture

Ascribe to the LORD, *O heavenly beings, / ascribe to the* LORD *glory and strength. / Ascribe to the* LORD *the glory of his name; / worship the* LORD *in holy splendor.... The* LORD *sits enthroned over the flood; / the* LORD *sits enthroned as king forever. / May the* LORD *give strength to his people! / May the* LORD *bless his people with peace!*   —Psalm 29:1-2, 10-11

Questions for Reflection

- What words come to mind to describe the character of God?

- What is your understanding of the "kingdom of God," and how was this understanding either confirmed or changed after reading and studying the assignments for this week?

Examining God's Word in Context

(20–30 minutes)

The Psalms claim that all of life belongs to the Lord and that God's reign extends over all creation.

Viewing the Video: Session 6, Part 1 (2:41)

The aim of Part 1 is to help participants experience a specific psalm (always one listed in the week's reading assignments) through spoken word,

34

music, and image and then invite both reflection and discussion. The recommended procedure for using this video is as follows: (1) **Preparation:** Group members should clear their minds in anticipation of receiving a new insight from a fresh hearing of God's Word. (2) **Attention:** Group members should listen meditatively to the psalm text (or texts) as they are presented either by recitation or through music, and pay attention to the images and how they illuminate the text of the psalm(s). (3) **Discussion:** Thoughtful discussion should follow careful listening. Use the following set of questions for guiding the group's responses.

Psalm 96
- After viewing this video segment, what would you say is the basic message of this psalm?

- What thoughts or feelings were evoked by the music and images that accompanied this psalm?

- Where in the context of worship would you expect to hear this psalm recited or sung? Why?

- When in your life have you found this psalm most meaningful?

Viewing the Video: Session 6, Part 2 (4:22)
The focus in this section is on viewing Part 2 of the video. Part 2 of each video will feature insights from one of two biblical scholars who will appear alternately in an informal interview format. They will talk about those psalms presented in the Part 1 segments, addressing such questions as:

- What can be inferred about the intent of the psalmist in this psalm?

- How might this psalm have been used by Israel in its worship?

- What does this psalm teach/say about God and God's relationship with people or the world?

- What particular characteristics of the psalm help articulate its message?

Prepare to View Video
Listen for what is said about the connection between Psalm 96 and the blues and about the meaning of the phrase *the Lord reigns.*

Discuss After Viewing Video

In this video segment, Old Testament scholar Stephen Reid discusses Psalm 96. On its own, the conversation may prompt sufficient discussion by the group. Simply following up the video with questions such as "What insight from the scholar caught your attention and why?" or "How did the discussion inform your understanding of the week's reading?" may be enough to start and sustain a discussion. Another option is to choose one or more of the four general questions above to prompt discussion of the video, or consider using the questions below:

- Why would it have been so important to Israel to sing a "renewing" song rather than a "new" song? What are some renewing songs we sing as Christian congregations? What purpose do they accomplish for us?

- Christians in North America today are not a marginalized people as were the Israelites living during the Babylonian exile period. Nonetheless, what aspects of feeling "dislocated" as a people do Christians experience today, causing us to want to sing the blues?

Encountering God's Word in the Text

(20–30 minutes)

We sense in the Psalms a struggle for the soul taking place as the Hebrew people live in the tension between the rule of kings and claim of the prophets. Worship of God without justice toward humanity is a sacrilege.

In the total group, hear Micah 6:6-8 and Psalm 20 read aloud, one passage right after the other.

Then form groups of three or four and invite each group to review their notes on the assignment for Day 5, which included reading several passages from the prophets. Have the groups share the responses they made to the questions in that assignment section (participant book, page 72): "What tensions do the prophets see between worship and ethical responsibility? How might acts of justice and mercy challenge or underscore the worship of God? What difference does it make that those who do justice and love mercy (act ethically) also walk humbly with their God (worship)?"

Next, still in groups of three or four, reread Psalm 98 and discuss the connections between worship, the reign of God, and the kingdom of God and how these connections are expressed in worship today. Call attention to the quote by James L. Mays in the marginal note on page 74 in the participant book. Have groups reflect on what it means for Mays to say that the integrity of psalmic speech depends on the proclamation "The LORD reigns."

If time allows, explore the week's readings from another perspective by considering the following statement: "Worship really matters . . . because worship is the place where creation's mute cries of praise are gathered up and uttered with a human voice" (participant book, pages 76–77). Talk together in the total group about what that statement means.

Finally, consider the following questions:

• How does the act of worship address the struggles of the soul? In what ways does the use of the Psalms in worship address the struggles of the soul?

Going Forth With God's Word: An Invitation to Discipleship

(15–20 minutes)

We do not reign over our own lives, and certainly not over the lives of our neighbors. One infinitely and eternally wiser, truer, and more compassionate than we are reigns supreme.

• What difference does it make in your life to know that the Lord reigns, not you?

• Where in your life do you need to allow God to reign supreme?

Call attention to the "For Reflection" section on page 78 in the participant book. Ask pairs to share responses to the questions.

Closing and Prayer

Turn to Session 7, and review the focus of the lesson and the assignments for the week ahead. Invite prayer concerns and pray together at this time.

Lament (and Praise)

Gathering Around God's Word

(5–10 minutes)

Welcome
   Begin on time by welcoming the group to the study.

Prayer
   Pray together as you begin your study. Consider using some of the prayers recorded in the Psalms, such as Psalm 44.

Invitation From Scripture
   How long, O LORD? Will you forget me forever? / How long will you hide your face from me? / How long must I bear pain in my soul, / and have sorrow in my heart all day long?...I trusted in your steadfast love; / my heart shall rejoice in your salvation. / I will sing to the LORD / because he has dealt bountifully with me.   *—Psalm 13:1-2a, 5-6*

Questions for Reflection
   • Why is transformation often the result of turbulence? When have you experienced significant change or transformation in your life following some trauma or trial?

   • Why do you avoid prayers of lament? How do prayers of lament call us to reclaim God's faithfulness?

Examining God's Word in Context

(20–30 minutes)

   The Psalms are distinctly Hebrew in so many ways, but at some level the psalms of lament reflect something common to all humanity.

Viewing the Video: Session 7, Part 1 (6:43)

The aim of Part 1 is to help participants experience a specific psalm (always one listed in the week's reading assignments) through spoken word, music, and image and then invite both reflection and discussion. The recommended procedure for using this video is as follows: (1) **Preparation:** Group members should clear their minds in anticipation of receiving a new insight from a fresh hearing of God's Word. (2) **Attention:** Group members should listen meditatively to the psalm text (or texts) as they are presented either by recitation or through music, and pay attention to the images and how they illuminate the text of the psalm(s). (3) **Discussion:** Thoughtful discussion should follow careful listening. Use the following set of questions for guiding the group's responses.

Psalm 22:1-22

- After viewing this video segment, what would you say is the basic message of this psalm?

- What thoughts or feelings were evoked by the music and images that accompanied this psalm?

- Where in the context of worship would you expect to hear this psalm recited or sung? Why?

- When in your life have you found this psalm most meaningful?

Note: Because this video segment is fairly long, you may want to alert the group before viewing it. Also, the text of the psalm you will hear chanted comes from the Psalter found in the Book of Common Prayer. It differs from the NRSV.

Viewing the Video: Session 7, Part 2 (5:33)

The focus in this section is on viewing Part 2 of the video. Part 2 of each video will feature insights from one of two biblical scholars who will appear alternately in an informal interview format. They will talk about those psalms presented in the Part 1 segments, addressing such questions as:

- What can be inferred about the intent of the psalmist in this psalm?

- How might this psalm have been used by Israel in its worship?

- What does this psalm teach/say about God and God's relationship with people or the world?

- What particular characteristics of the psalm help articulate its message?

Prepare to View Video
Listen for what is said about Psalm 22 as representative of the psalms of lament, what Jesus meant by quoting Psalm 22:1 from the cross, and what a psalm of lament says about God.

Discuss After Viewing Video
In this video segment, Old Testament scholar Julia O'Brien discusses Psalm 22. On its own, the conversation may prompt sufficient discussion by the group. Simply following up the video with questions such as "What insight from the scholar caught your attention and why?" or "How did the discussion inform your understanding of the week's reading?" may be enough to start and sustain a discussion. Another option is to choose one or more of the four general questions above to prompt discussion of the video, or consider using the questions below:

- What does it say about the faith of the psalmists that a third of the psalms are laments?

- What is the value of praying or singing a lament as a community rather than as an individual?

- What difference does it make in your view of Jesus' death on the cross to think that Jesus intended his hearers to remember all of Psalm 22, even though he only spoke verse 1?

Encountering God's Word in the Text

(20–30 minutes)

The psalms of lament stand as a testimony of those innocent victims of history who suffer violence and exile, and who raise their fist toward heaven demanding God's justice in the face of human cruelty.

Form five groups and assign each group one of the five days' readings (example: **Group 1**—Day 1 readings). Have each group choose one of the psalms from the assigned day's readings and trace the movement of the psalm according to the pattern suggested by Walter Brueggemann (see participant book, pages 85–87). Note (1) the *past orientation* in which life and faith were settled and taken for granted; (2) the *disorientation* when danger and loss overtake the psalmist; and (3) finally, the *new orientation* where faith must expand or be transformed to take account of God's purposes in light of the difficulties faced.

Allow time for groups to share the movement they identified in their chosen psalm.

Then have everyone locate Psalm 80 and note the call-and-response pattern of the text. Enlist one person in the group to read aloud only the three call sections of the psalm (verses 1-2, 4-6, 8-18), and have the whole group together read the responses in verses 3, 7, and 19. Following the reading, ask each individual to create his or her own prayer of lament, using the pattern of Psalm 80.

Invite those who are willing to share with the total group what they have written. Then talk about how a psalm of lament maps the course of a life transformed in a crucible of suffering.

• How do our experiences of suffering change our understanding of God's relationship to the world and our relationship to God?

Going Forth With God's Word: An Invitation to Discipleship

(15–20 minutes)

The psalms of lament exist because people of faith—people who trust God, people who know the story of God's faithfulness as their own history—refuse to close their eyes to the world around them.

• What are ways that you keep your eyes open to the world around you?

• What trials of life have brought you into a closer relationship with God? How did you respond? How did you see God respond?

Call attention to the "For Reflection" section on page 89 in the participant book. Ask pairs to share responses to the questions.

Closing and Prayer

Turn to Session 8, and review the focus of the lesson and the assignments for the week ahead. Invite prayer concerns and pray together at this time.

Grace and Repentance

Gathering Around God's Word

(5–10 minutes)

Welcome
Begin on time by welcoming the group to the study.

Prayer
Pray together as you begin your study. Consider using some of the prayers recorded in the Psalms, such as Psalm 6.

Invitation From Scripture
Have mercy on me, O God, / according to your steadfast love; / according to your abundant mercy / blot out my transgressions. / Wash me thoroughly from my iniquity, / and cleanse me from my sin. / For I know my transgressions, / and my sin is ever before me. —Psalm 51:1-3

Questions for Reflection
- How would you describe your experience with the Penitential Service each day this past week?

- After this week's readings, how would you define the words *grace* and *repentance*?

Examining God's Word in Context

(20–30 minutes)

Repentance includes remorse, our feeling sorry for our sin. But repentance is much more than that. It means to turn around, to turn fully from one direction to another. Repentance requires surrender to God's direction for our lives.

Viewing the Video: Session 8, Part 1 (6:35)
The aim of Part 1 is to help participants experience a specific psalm (always one listed in the week's reading assignments) through spoken word,

music, and image and then invite both reflection and discussion. The rec-ommended procedure for using this video is as follows: (1) **Preparation:** Group members should clear their minds in anticipation of receiving a new insight from a fresh hearing of God's Word. (2) **Attention:** Group members should listen meditatively to the psalm text (or texts) as they are presented either by recitation or through music, and pay attention to the images and how they illuminate the text of the psalm(s). (3) **Discussion:** Thoughtful discussion should follow careful listening. Use the following set of ques-tions for guiding the group's responses.

Psalm 51

• After viewing this video segment, what would you say is the basic mes-sage of this psalm?

• What thoughts or feelings were evoked by the music and images that accompanied this psalm?

• Where in the context of worship would you expect to hear this psalm recited or sung? Why?

• When in your life have you found this psalm most meaningful?

Note: Because the video segment is fairly long, you may want to alert the group before viewing it. Also, because the musical setting of Psalm 51 is Allegri's "Miserere," the NRSV text of the psalm will be displayed on screen.

Viewing the Video: Session 8, Part 2 (5:50)

The focus in this section is on viewing Part 2 of the video. Part 2 of each video will feature insights from one of two biblical scholars who will appear alternately in an informal interview format. They will talk about those psalms presented in the Part 1 segments, addressing such questions as:

• What can be inferred about the intent of the psalmist in this psalm?

• How might this psalm have been used by Israel in its worship?

• What does this psalm teach/say about God and God's relationship with people or the world?

• What particular characteristics of the psalm help articulate its message?

Prepare to View Video

Listen what is said about David as a "celebrity" penitent and what the terms *heart* and *sacrifice* mean in the context of Psalm 51.

Discuss After Viewing Video

In this video segment, Old Testament scholar Stephen Reid discusses Psalm 51. On its own, the conversation may prompt sufficient discussion by the group. Simply following up the video with questions such as "What insight from the scholar caught your attention and why?" or "How did the discussion inform your understanding of the week's reading?" may be enough to start and sustain a discussion. Another option is to choose one or more of the four general questions above to prompt discussion of the video, or consider using the questions below:

- According to a penitential psalm like Psalm 51, what actions and attitudes are necessary to be truly penitent?

- What does Psalm 51 say about who God is and about our relationship with God?

- What barriers often keep us from opening our eyes to our need for reconciliation with God?

Encountering God's Word in the Text

(20–30 minutes)

The penitential psalms help us understand the personal dimensions of sin by the various shades of meaning they convey. In the total group, discuss the differences in meaning of the following words: *transgression*, *iniquity*, and *sin*.

Now lead the group in the opening sections of the Penitential Service printed on pages 92–94 in the participant book. Read the Opening Sentences and observe the brief silent reflections. Read the Call to Worship and Prayer and follow that by singing the first stanza of "Great Is Thy Faithfulness."

Next, form four groups and make the following assignments:

    Group 1: Psalm 102 and Isaiah 58

    Group 2: Psalm 32 and Luke 15

    Group 3: Psalm 143 and Luke 18

    Group 4: Psalm 130 and Romans 3:9-26

Call the groups' attention to the first paragraph under the "Invitation to Discipleship" section in the participant book (page 103) and to the notion that the penitential psalms are concerned with what it means to learn how to live. Then instruct each group to determine: (a) what the psalm says about how to live and (b) how the other Scripture supports or expands on what the psalm says.

As a wrap-up activity, invite each person to say what the word *repentance* means, after having now read the week's Scriptures and experienced the Penitential Service each day.

Finally, lead the total group in the closing sections of the Penitential Service printed on pages 94–96 in the participant book. Read the Call to Confession and the Prayer of Confession with the group responding accordingly. Sing one stanza of "Amazing Grace." Pray the Closing Prayer.

Going Forth With God's Word: An Invitation to Discipleship

(15–20 minutes)

We are called to bow before God, who alone is holy and righteous, who alone judges rightly, and to confess our sin to God and in the presence of one another.

- As a sinner forgiven by the mercy of God, when have you experienced God's mercy yourself or seen God's mercy at work in the life of someone else?

- How would you say acts of repentance and assurances of God's grace have made you not more religious but more human?

Call attention to the "For Reflection" section on page 104 in the participant book. Ask pairs to share responses to the questions.

Closing and Prayer

Turn to Session 9, and review the focus of the lesson and the assignments for the week ahead. Invite prayer concerns and pray together at this time.

Love and Wrath

(5–10 minutes)

Welcome

Begin on time by welcoming the group to the study.

Prayer

Pray together as you begin your study. Consider using some of the prayers recorded in the Psalms, such as Psalm 69.

Invitation From Scripture

O LORD, you God of vengeance, / you God of vengeance, shine forth! / Rise up, O judge of the earth; / give to the proud what they deserve! —Psalm 94:1-2

Questions for Reflection

- What feelings did the readings this week evoke for you?

- How do you deal with the tension between God's wrath and God's love?

Examining God's Word in Context

(20–30 minutes)

Viewing the Video: Session 9, Part 1 (3:52)

The aim of Part 1 is to help participants experience a specific psalm (always one listed in the week's reading assignments) through spoken word, music, and image and then invite both reflection and discussion. The recommended procedure for using this video is as follows: (1) **Preparation:** Group members should clear their minds in anticipation of receiving a new insight from a fresh hearing of God's Word. (2) **Attention:** Group members should listen meditatively to the psalm text (or texts) as they are presented either by recitation or through music, and pay attention to the images and how they illuminate the text of the psalm(s). (3) **Discussion:** Thoughtful discussion should follow careful listening. Use the following set of questions for guiding the group's responses.

Psalm 94
- After viewing this video segment, what would you say is the basic message of this psalm?

- What thoughts or feelings were evoked by the music and images that accompanied this psalm?

- Where in the context of worship would you expect to hear this psalm recited or sung? Why?

- When in your life have you found this psalm most meaningful?

Viewing the Video: Session 9, Part 2 (4:34)
The focus in this section is on viewing Part 2 of the video. Part 2 of each video will feature insights from one of two biblical scholars who will appear alternately in an informal interview format. They will talk about those psalms presented in the Part 1 segments, addressing such questions as:

- What can be inferred about the intent of the psalmist in this psalm?

- How might this psalm have been used by Israel in its worship?

- What does this psalm teach/say about God and God's relationship with people or the world?

- What particular characteristics of the psalm help articulate its message?

Prepare to View Video
Listen for insights into the relationship between the psalmist's cry for vengeance and God's justice.

Discuss After Viewing Video
In this video segment, Old Testament scholar Julia O'Brien discusses Psalm 94. On its own, the conversation may prompt sufficient discussion by the group. Simply following up the video with questions such as "What insight from the scholar caught your attention and why?" or "How did the discussion inform your understanding of the week's reading?" may be

enough to start and sustain a discussion. Another option is to choose one or more of the four general questions above to prompt discussion of the video, or consider using the questions below:

- What makes a text like Psalm 94 so difficult for you to hear and understand?

- In what ways do you think Christians today might be a part of the oppression of the widow, the stranger, and the orphan?

- Dr. O'Brien suggests that Christian readers take responsibility for how they interpret biblical texts, especially ones like the psalms of vengeance. How do you do that?

Encountering God's Word in the Text

(20–30 minutes)

To say that God loves us is to say that God is freely and completely for us. God loves us simply because of who God is: God is love.

One option for exploring this week's readings is to follow the instructions for the "Daily Assignments" section of the participant book (page 106). Take each day's Scripture readings and discuss them using the three bulleted questions as indicated.

Another approach is to use a single psalm as the basis for discussion in the following manner: Hear Psalm 35 read aloud in the total group. Talk together about what insights came from the readings this week regarding the wrath of God. Then focus the group's discussion on the following questions:

- In light of how you see the world, what does the wrath of humanity look like, and what causes it? Give specific examples.

- According to the psalmists, what does the wrath of God look like, and what causes it?

- How would you compare and contrast the wrath of humanity and the wrath of God?

- How does justice and righteousness fit into the wrath of God? How does justice and righteousness fit into the love of God? Read Isaiah 11 and talk about how that text addresses those two questions.

For a third option, form two groups. Assign Group 1 the psalm and Gospel readings for Day 4 and Group 2 the psalms and Gospel readings for Day 5. Instruct the two groups to recall the readings and review any notes they have on them. Then have them identify the central message of the psalm(s) and the central message of Jesus' teachings. How do the messages compare? How do you reconcile the messages? How do these messages speak to the command to "love your enemies"?

Going Forth With God's Word: An Invitation to Discipleship

(15–20 minutes)

The reason we are called to love our enemies is because the Lord reigns over us and over them. We all belong to the Lord, and we bear witness to the character of the Lord to whom we belong precisely by loving our enemies—even when we feel vengeful toward them.

- Why is it so difficult to return good for evil?

- In your experience, how have you typically responded to your enemies—with wrath or with love? When is wrath appropriate? What are ways that you love your enemies?

Call attention to the "For Reflection" section on page 115 in the participant book. Ask pairs to share responses to the questions.

Closing and Prayer

Turn to Session 10, and review the focus of the lesson and the assignments for the week ahead. Invite prayer concerns and pray together at this time.

progressive revelation

awareness of God's justice + sin intolerance

Hallelujah and Amen

Gathering Around God's Word

(5–10 minutes)

Welcome
Begin on time by welcoming the group to the study.

Prayer
Pray together as you begin your study. Consider using some of the prayers recorded in the Psalms, such as Psalm 100.

Invitation From Scripture
Praise the LORD! / How good it is to sing praises to our God; / for he is gracious, and a song of praise is fitting.... Sing to the LORD with thanksgiving; / make melody to our God on the lyre. —Psalm 147:1, 7

Questions for Reflection
- How do you express your praise to God for all that God has done?

- How can praise to God provide you with fullness in life?

Examining God's Word in Context

(20–30 minutes)

The psalms of praise reflect the fullness of human life for which we were created. They inhale the creative life of God and exhale gratitude and praise.

Viewing the Video: Session 10, Part 1 (3:22)
The aim of Part 1 is to help participants experience a specific psalm (always one listed in the week's reading assignments) through spoken word, music, and image and then invite both reflection and discussion. The recommended procedure for using this video is as follows: (1) **Preparation:** Group members should clear their minds in anticipation of receiving a new insight from a fresh hearing of God's Word. (2) **Attention:** Group members

should listen meditatively to the psalm text (or texts) as they are presented either by recitation or through music, and pay attention to the images and how they illuminate the text of the psalm(s). (3) **Discussion:** Thoughtful discussion should follow careful listening. Use the following set of questions for guiding the group's responses.

Psalms 146 & 150

- After viewing this video segment, what would you say is the basic message of each of these psalms?

- What thoughts or feelings were evoked by the music and images that accompanied these psalms?

- Where in the context of worship would you expect to hear these psalms recited or sung? Why?

- When in your life have you found these psalms most meaningful?

Viewing the Video: Session 10, Part 2

The focus in this section is on viewing Part 2 of the video. Part 2 of each video will feature insights from one of two biblical scholars who will appear alternately in an informal interview format. They will talk about those psalms presented in the Part 1 segments, addressing such questions as:

- What can be inferred about the intent of the psalmist in this psalm?

- How might this psalm have been used by Israel in its worship?

- What does this psalm teach/say about God and God's relationship with people or the world?

- What particular characteristics of the psalm help articulate its message?

Prepare to View Video

Listen for ways in which the psalms connect us with the world and lead us into full-bodied praise.

Discuss After Viewing Video

In this video segment, Old Testament scholar Stephen Reid discusses Psalms 146 and 150. On its own, the conversation may prompt sufficient discussion by the group. Simply following up the video with questions such as "What insight from the scholar caught your attention and why?" or "How did the discussion inform your understanding of the week's reading?" may be enough to start and sustain a discussion. Another option is to choose one or more of the four general questions above to prompt discussion of the video, or consider using the questions below:

- What is your understanding of the transforming power of God in creation? In the world? In the church? In an individual's life? How do the Psalms address this transforming power?

- Throughout this study of the Psalms, we have looked at the connection between culture and faith. How is this connection played out in the world today? In the church? How can you be a bridge between culture and faith in your own life?

- Psalm 150 calls every component of the universe to praise the Lord. What transformation do you see happening in the world if this call became a reality? What transformation do you see happening in your church if this call became a reality?

Encountering God's Word in the Text

(20–30 minutes)

The Psalms challenge us to see the world through eyes enlarged by eternity and to see in this world all that makes it holy, mysterious, and wonderful because it belongs to God.

In the total group, sing (or recite) one stanza of the hymn "Holy, Holy, Holy! Lord God Almighty." Read Psalm 147 and discuss the elements of praise found in the psalm.

- What elements of praise do you experience in corporate worship at your church?

- What elements of praise do you experience in your personal worship or devotional time?

Form groups of three or four. Instruct each group to focus on the reading assignment for Day 2 and answer the following questions:

- What characteristics of God are found in these readings? What characteristics would you add from other readings? What is your understanding of God based on these characteristics?

The psalms of praise map out a new direction for us. They make clear the purposes and ends for which God created us. Still in the same groups of three or four, use notes and the readings for Day 5 to discuss the journey into God's promised future.

- What do you think God's promised future looks like? What does the road look like that will take us there? How are the two paths described in Psalm 1 both a guiding principle for the Book of Psalms and our guide into God's promised future?

In the total group, sing (or recite) a stanza of "Praise to the Lord, the Almighty."

Going Forth With God's Word: An Invitation to Discipleship

(15–20 minutes)

The Psalms teach us to make our lives into living "hallelujahs" and "amens" spoken to the God who reigns. The Psalms invite us to praise and love God for who God is rather than to love the little images of God we have made in our own likeness.

- Share a hallelujah moment in your life.

- The Psalms call us to share the character of the God we worship. Which characteristics of God would you like to share in your life?

- How do you plan to allow your heart to be transformed resulting in a life of living hallelujahs and amens?

Call attention to the last question in the "For Reflection" section on page 126 in the participant book. Use that question as the basis for the group's closing reflection on the Psalms and on the study.

Closing and Prayer

Thank the group members for their participation. Make any announcements that are needed. Consider singing or reciting the words to a hymn based on a psalm as part of the closing. Some recommended hymns are:

"The Lord's My Shepherd, I'll Not Want" (Psalm 23)

"Joy to the World" (Psalm 98)

"O Worship the King" (Psalm 104)

"Thy Word Is a Lamp" (Psalm 119)

Then close in prayer. Consider reading Romans 16:25-27 to end the prayer.

Video Credits

Opening Sequence

Artwork: *David Singing*, by James Tissot (1836–1902 / French), Jewish Museum, New York, USA, © SuperStock, Inc. / SuperStock. ❖ *The shepherd*, by Charles Wellington Furse (1868–1904), Bourne Gallery, Reigate, Great Britain, Fine Art Photographic Library, London / Art Resource, NY.

Photography: © SuperStock, Inc. / SuperStock.

Session 1—Psalms 1 & 23

Photography: © SuperStock, Inc. / SuperStock.

Readers: Mark Cabus: Psalm 1; Nan Gurley: Psalm 23.

Music: Psalm 1: Organ improvisation, Gerry Senechal, organist, St. George's Episcopal Church, Nashville, TN.

Music: Psalm 23: Anglican chant, arr. K. J. Pye: Psalm 23; performed by St. George's Choir, Nashville, TN; Dr. Murray Forbes Somerville, Director of Music.

Session 2—Psalm 136:1-16, 26

Images of outer space from the Hubble Space Telescope provided courtesy of NASA and STScI.

Artwork: *God Dividing the Waters & Earth* Fresco, Michelangelo Buonarroti (1475–1564 / Italian), Sistine Chapel, Vatican, © SuperStock, Inc. / SuperStock. ❖ *Chaos (the Creation)* 1841, I. Aywasovski (1817–1900 / Armenian), Armenian Museum, Venice, © SuperStock, Inc. / SuperStock. ❖ *Sunrise on the Sea*, 1872, John Frederick Kensett (1816–1872 / American), Oil on canvas, Metropolitan Museum of Art, New York City, NY, USA, © SuperStock, Inc. / SuperStock. ❖ *Starry Night*, 1889, Vincent van Gogh (1853–1890 / Dutch), Oil on canvas, © SuperStock, Inc. / SuperStock. ❖ *Seven Plagues of Egypt: Exodus. Angel of the Lord, sword in hand, leaving mothers lamenting the death of the first born.* Illustration by Gustave Dore (1832–1883), French painter and book illustrator for "The Bible" (London 1866). Wood engraving. © Image Asset Management Ltd. / SuperStock. ❖ *Pharaoh Pursues The Israelites*, by James Tissot (1836–1902 / French), Jewish Museum, New York City, © SuperStock, Inc. / SuperStock. ❖ *The Exodus*, by James Tissot

(1836–1902 / French), Jewish Museum, New York City, © SuperStock, Inc. / SuperStock. ❖ *Moses Divides the Waters of the Red Sea*, by Christoffer W. Eckersberg (1783–1853 / Danish), © SuperStock, Inc. / SuperStock. ❖ *Death of the Egyptians in the Red Sea*, 1625–27, by Matthäus Merian the elder (1593–1650 / Swiss), Copperplate, © SuperStock, Inc. / SuperStock.

Readers: Mark Cabus, Matthew B. Carlton.

Session 3—Psalms 42 & 43

Photography: © SuperStock, Inc. / SuperStock.

Reader: Denice Hicks.

Session 4—Psalm 27

Photography: © SuperStock, Inc. / SuperStock.

Music: Plainsong chant, Tone II.I; performed by St. George's Choir, Nashville, TN; Dr. Murray Forbes Somerville, Director of Music.

Session 5—Psalm 19

Photography: © SuperStock, Inc. / SuperStock.

Reader: Matthew B. Carlton.

Session 6—Psalm 96

Photography: © SuperStock, Inc. / SuperStock.

Artwork: *The Songs of Joy*, by James J. Tissot (1836–1902 / French), Jewish Museum, New York, © SuperStock, Inc. / SuperStock. ❖ *Orange*, 1994, by Elizabeth Heuer (20th C. American), Collage Collection of the Artist, © Elizabeth Heuer / SuperStock ❖ *Negro Spirituals II*, by Leslie Xuereb (b.1959 / French), © Leslie Xuereb / SuperStock.

Reader: Nan Gurley.

Session 7—Psalm 22:1-22

Photography: Tim Campbell.

Actor: Mark Cabus.

Cantor: Timothy O. Fudge.

Music: Plainsong chant

Session 8—Psalm 51

Artwork: *David Singing*, by James Tissot (1836–1902 / French), Jewish Museum, New York, USA, © SuperStock, Inc. / SuperStock.

Photography: © SuperStock, Inc. / SuperStock.

Music: "Miserere," by Gregorio Allegri, adapted and arranged for English use by Ivor Atkins, ©1951, Novello & Company, Ltd., performed by St. George's Choir, Nashville, TN; Dr. Murray Forbes Somerville, Director of Music; Zoe Harkin, soprano; Caroline Peyton, mezzo; Michelle Cox, alto; Jesse Turner, bass.

Session 9—Psalm 94

Photography: © SuperStock, Inc. / SuperStock. ❖ *Migrant Mother*, Nipomo, California, USA, 1936. Photographed by Dorothea Lange, © Culver Pictures, Inc. / SuperStock.

Reader: Stella Reed.

Session 10—Psalms 146 & 150

Photography: © SuperStock, Inc. / SuperStock.

Readers: Denice Hicks: Psalm 146; Mark Cabus: Psalm 150.

Music: Psalm 146: Chant from the Ionian Psalter, by Peter R. Hallock, ©1986, Ionian Arts, Inc., performed by St. George's Choir, Nashville, TN; Dr. Murray Forbes Somerville, Director of Music.

Music: Psalm 150: Organ improvisation; Gerry Senechal, organist; St. George's Episcopal Church, Nashville, TN.